D1395458

"I don't believe it!"

"I don't believe it!"

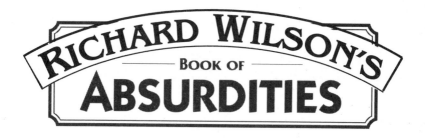

RICHARD WILSON'S
BOOK OF
ABSURDITIES

Illustrations by
Martin Honeysett

Michael O'Mara Books Limited

First published in 1995 by
Michael O'Mara Books Limited
9 Lion Yard, Tremadoc Road
London SW4 7NQ

A CIP catalogue record for this book is available from the British Library.

ISBN 1-85479-620-8

Designed by Robert Updegraff
Printed and bound in Finland by WSOY

Hello!

Welcome to this collection of 'Absurdities'. I think David Renwick, the brilliant writer of *One Foot in the Grave*, would agree with me when I say that, 'I don't believe it!' was never intended as a catch phrase. It just sort of happened.

Victor Meldrew said it quite frequently of course; then the public latched on to it and then the press. Now a somewhat tired old exclamation has been revitalized and seems to epitomize Victor's view of life.

David Renwick does claim that most of the things that happen in the programme are based on fact. It is my job, as an actor, to make them believable.

I have always been fascinated by the extraordinary 'fabric' of the human condition and pride myself in having a nose for what is true and what isn't.

Everything in this book has been authenticated so it's no good you saying, 'I don't believe it!' Yes, it's all true – the rich, wonderful world of human absurdity!

Let's start with what makes us all most absurd – love and sex.

Love, Sex, Women and the Whole Damned Thing!

I suppose I'm a bit old fashioned, but really, when I see two teenagers identically dressed – or rather undressed – snogging away in public, I wonder at how it has all changed so much for the worse since I was a teenager. In my day, if we took a girl out on a date we dressed up; now you can't even tell which sex is which – both of them garbed in their filthy jeans and what-have-you, doing things to each other I would have considered to be medically impossible. I just hope they don't scare the horses. They certainly scare me. As I said to one youth sitting on our garden wall with his tongue down his girlfriend's throat – if I needed to get food that badly I'd use a tin opener.

But what is sexually 'normal' when there are so many contradictory ideas of how the sexes should behave. Perhaps I should like it in India where, I'm reliably informed, the first kiss on the cinema screen happened as recently as 1978 and even then caused outrage. It's certainly better than America where, as Bob Hope said: 'They're doing things on the screen today that I wouldn't do in bed . . . if I could!'

And not just on the silver screen . . . In 1984, in a mouth-to-mouth marathon, a couple spent 17 days and 10 $1/2$ hours locked in labial contact. Yuk! It's all a long way from when Chico Marx said, 'I wasn't kissing her, I was just whispering in her mouth!'

I don't believe it!

———— • ————

Nobody's been able to define love satisfactorily. One thing it *isn't* is the definition supplied by the International Conference on Love and Attraction: 'The cognitive-affective state characterized by intrusive and obsessive fantasizing concerning reciprocity and amorant feeling by the object of amorance.' Phew!

In the Middle Ages even women's ears were deemed erogenous zones and had to be kept covered. The trouble with love is that it so often leads to marriage – though not always a long marriage. There are a million honeymoon disaster stories but the one about poor Mr Philip Ryan should stand as a warning to young men everywhere. It was in 1977 and, to impress his new wife, he vaulted over the fence which surrounded his holiday bungalow. Unfortunately he forgot that on the other side of the fence was a deep volcano. He plunged down 500 feet and was killed. The shortest wedding on record however, is that of Robert Neiderhiser who breathed his last in Pennsylvania, only moments after whispering, 'I do' at the altar rails.

Another brief honeymoon was enjoyed by the film star Eva Gabor. Her third marriage was to plastic surgeon John Williams. 'After we were married one minute, I wanted to leave him,' she said. Even worse was Marisa Carlotta who met an old flame at her wedding, chatted to him for a while and, realizing she still loved him, took off with him there and then to New York.

Katherine Mansfield, the New Zealand writer, enjoyed a longer honeymoon – until she reached the honeymoon hotel in fact. Not liking the decor, she vamoosed. The heiress, Barbara Hutton, married a good deal as millionaires are inclined to do. On one honeymoon she divested herself of her wedding garments to slip into something more comfortable. The marriage never recovered from her new husband's first comment: 'Barbara, you're too fat!'

A Scottish couple, Ian and Anne Marie Coombe, had problems of a different kind on their honeymoon. Anne Marie had a very possessive dog, a black-and-white Collie named Shep. 'Everything was fine until we went to bed,' said Anne Marie later. 'As Ian began to put his arms around me, Shep went mad and leaped onto the bed to part us. Ian thought he was kidding until Shep gave a ferocious growl, showed his teeth and prepared to pounce. Every time Ian tried to touch me Shep grew nastier and the more I tried to calm him the angrier he got. In the end we gave up. With Ian pinned to

*"I knew it was a mistake,
bringing him on our honeymoon."*

the wall by Shep, I had one of the quietest honey-moon nights on record!'

Oddly enough the Emperor Napoleon had the same experience. As he made love to Josephine on their wedding night, her pet pug, believing her to be under attack, leapt onto the bed and bit Napoleon on the buttocks. All-in-all, wedding nights can be a pain in the fundament.

In-laws can be a problem too. Allen Farber of Chicago divorced his wife after she denied him access to her bed. He then sued his former in-laws because his ex-wife's mother had warned her not to have any children by him in case they were born with their father's looks.

Some people are obsessed with the whole idea of marriage and that's not healthy! Adrienne Cuyot was engaged 652 times and married 53 times over a period of 23 years.

The Russians enjoy their weddings and it was reported that, in 1980, the mayor of Leningrad threw a wonderful reception for his daughter's wedding. He even persuaded the city's great museum, the Hermitage, to lend a tea-set made for Catherine the Great. Unfortunately, one guest dropped his cup and, other guests thinking this was the start of the traditional toast, got to their feet and threw their cups at the wall – a smashing time was had by all!

However good Russian wedding parties may be, Russian marriages aren't always so successful. In 1995 *Cosmopolitan*, the women's magazine, carried out the first sex survey in Russia and discovered that over half Russia's married women have been unfaithful to their husbands.

In February 1981, a 28-year-old Indonesian was jailed for seven years – his offence? He had been married to 121 women since 1974. In mitigation he pointed out that he had divorced 93 of them!

So far the oldest couple to divorce are Ida Stern and her husband Simon. In 1984 they filed for divorce even though Ida was 91 and Simon was 97. I suppose it's never too late to begin a new life.

Better divorce than murder: in Miami, a 90-year-old man was charged with killing his 76-year-old bride of less than a week during an argument over whether they should or shouldn't take a honeymoon cruise.

As Dorothy Parker once said, 'I require only three things in a man: he must be handsome, ruthless – and stupid!'

Maybe divorce is the wrong approach to an unsatisfactory marriage. Right up until 1890 wives

were put up for sale by their husbands. Usually
the wife, with a rope round her neck, was led
round the market place by her husband and then
sold to the highest bidder. In 1797 the price of a
good wife was about threepence but *The Times*
reported on 22 July that 'the increasing value of
the fairer sex is considered by various celebrated
writers to be a sure sign of increasing civilization'!

I really can't agree with the eighteenth century
female dramatist, Hannah Cowley who declared:
'What is woman? Only one of Nature's agreeable
blunders.' Agreeable, yes but not a blunder.

As far as sex is concerned, women are by far the
cleverer. According to a survey carried out by
Shere Hite, over half of the women interviewed
claimed they faked orgasms. To quote one woman:
'For fifteen years I was the world's best faker.
Honestly, they should have a phallic trophy
mounted on a pedestal for all women – I think
they all fake with men.'

Perhaps Dr Belkin is right after all. Writing in a
Russian medical journal, he ruled that the correct
duration for sexual intercourse is . . . two minutes.

———— • ————

And what happens if you stay married? Before you can say 'Oh my God', your wife gets pregnant. When a gentleman called Morgan Lamb failed his exams for the Los Angeles bar, he got his wife to impersonate him for the re-sits. The ruse worked in the sense that his better half got him the grades he needed but one of the examiners spotted something a bit suspicious about 'Mr' Lamb. Not surprising really: 'he' was seven months pregnant!

A British Airways stewardess had an unusual sexual arrangement with her husband before she left on short trips. To satisfy his penchant for bondage she would leave him tied up and naked in the bedroom wardrobe, returning to release him after the six-hour return journey to Paris. Everything went well until one day, in August 1984, when the plane was delayed in Paris for 24 hours. There was nothing for it: she had to ring the Metropolitan Police who broke into his apartment and released him.

I have to say it: **'I don't believe it!'**

"Apparently she wasn't expecting to be away for so long."

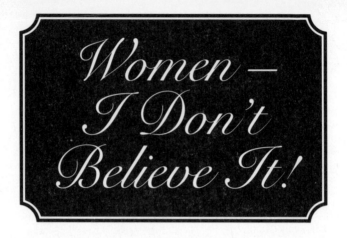

I have always enjoyed lists. Here is the
first of several lists in this book.

———— • ————

The women of the Tiwi tribe in the South Pacific
are forced to marry at birth.

———— • ————

The women of northern Siberia express affection for
their menfolk by showering them with lice and slugs.

In the sixteenth century women used to tie holly to the ends of their beds to stop them becoming witches.

———— • ————

Nero's wife had 500 asses at her disposal to keep her bath continually topped up with fresh milk.

———— • ————

According to university researchers in Arizona beautiful women have less self-confidence than plain Janes because being constantly ogled by men leads to anxiety (and in many cases pregnancy).

I don't really believe that!

According to an old Memphis by-law, a female must not drive an automobile unless she is preceded by a man waving a red flag.

———— • ————

A famous evangelist, Aimee McPherson, was buried with a telephone in her coffin so that she could contact the living world from beyond the grave. (After seven years without her making a call, the line was disconnected).

———— • ————

There was once a Scottish prostitute whose body was sold for dissection after she was murdered but the doctor who bought it was so impressed with it that he kept it preserved . . . in whisky.

"And not so fast this time."

In Italy a local law forbids women christened Mary to work as prostitutes.

———— • ————

According to The *Lancet*, the respected medical journal, in 1983 there was a New York hooker who had 15,000 clients. She only worked for three months of the year but when on duty had an estimated 24 clients a day. Ouch!

———— • ————

Many people enjoy being famous or even notorious but there are lengths to which only the most brazen will go. Take, for example, the case of Mary Tofts.

Mary Tofts was the wife of a cloth worker and lived in Godalming, Surrey. In 1726 she gave birth to a rabbit – or so *she* said. She was certainly pregnant when she admitted to craving for rabbit to eat but because she was very poor she could not get any.

As her time approached she dreamed constantly of rabbits and finally gave birth not just to one rabbit but to 20. She convinced her doctor, a Mr Howard, that this was no trick and soon her fame had spread far and wide.

King George I was one who believed in her and sent down his doctor, Mr Ahlers, who was so convinced that she had indeed given birth to rabbits that he promised to obtain a pension for her. At last she was brought to London where she was examined by a panel of distinguished doctors, many of whom believed her story. Indeed, only under the threat of torture could she be made to admit she was a fraud but can one believe a confession extracted under duress?

——— • ———

Researchers doing a survey on the sex industry in Copenhagen, Denmark, found a woman aged 66 stripping to supplement her pension, which shows that age and beauty *can* go together!

———— • ————

The first human cannon-ball was a woman. Her 60-foot flight caused such a sensation she made a living out of it.

———— • ————

The IQ range is wider among men than women. In other words scientists believe that the smartest men are smarter than the smartest women but the stupidest men are stupider.

Mrs Marva Drew of Iowa took five years to type out all the numbers from one to a million after her son's teacher said it wasn't possible.

———— • ————

A French magazine which conducted a poll into the nation's sex life discovered that French men admitted to sleeping with 11.2 women whereas French women admitted to sleeping with only 1.8 men.

———— • ————

In 1984 the Paris-Venice Orient Express ground to a halt and was delayed for almost an hour after a woman got her foot stuck in the emergency brake . . . while making love.

The first person to attempt crossing Niagara Falls in a barrel was a woman . . . who couldn't swim.

———— • ————

A survey in New York revealed that the average Manhattan wife takes 14 minutes to switch off the light after going to bed.

———— • ————

Under Italian law a woman convicted of minor offences could not be imprisoned if she were pregnant. When Eliga Spinelli was convicted of stealing a chicken in 1975 she was sentenced to ten months in jail. She avoided going to jail by becoming pregnant. She continued having children every year, totting up a record 14 babies by 1987.

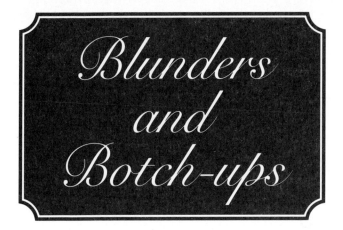

Blunders and Botch-ups

It is always nice to read about other people's blunders. I keep my own private!

———— • ————

Prisoners in Mexico planned a daring escape. They dug a tunnel without any of the guards noticing and one night scrambled through it to . . . well, not freedom exactly. They came up in the court in which they had been sentenced!

I Don't Believe It!

In January 1987 a woman was driving her car in Chester. She noticed how friendly people were waving at her as she passed by. At last she got the feeling that something might be wrong. It was! She was driving on the frozen Shropshire Union Canal. She just managed to get out of the car before it sank through the ice.

———— • ————

In Sicily, Antonio Percelli was being buried in a Palermo graveyard when, without warning, he jumped out of his coffin alive and well. However, his mother-in-law got such a shock she died of a heart attack and was buried in his place.

John Dillinger, the gangster, decided to get himself new fingerprints to confuse the FBI. He dipped his fingertips in acid and in great pain waited for the skin to heal. Unfortunately for him when the skin had grown again he discovered his fingerprints were the same as they had been before!

———— • ————

In 1983 the new Paris telephone directory was published. It was the triumphant product of modern computer technology and the French Telecommunications Ministry was very proud of it. That is until they consulted it and noticed that their own number was wrong!

I don't believe it!

I Don't Believe It!

A fisherman on the Arral Sea was enjoying the calm weather and the warm sun when his peace was disturbed by a flying cow. Out of the blue this Friesian landed on his boat destroying it and almost drowning him. Of course no one believed him and his adventure was thought to be a practical joke. The insurance company refused to pay him for his boat and it was even reported in the newspapers that he told the tallest of stories. Until, that is, the US Airforce admitted that a cow in one of their huge transport planes had gone mad and had been jettisoned over the Arral Sea!

I don't know much about money. It's jolly nice to have a bit, but I've no interest in making a great deal of it. Especially when experts tell you they can make you a fortune and *you* don't have to do a thing. Sometimes they get it wrong!

———— • ————

Honesty is always the best policy . . . or nearly always.

A jockey was due to ride the favourite at York. Just before the race a shady looking man offered him a suitcase full of money if the favourite lost. The jockey contemptuously refused to have anything to do with it. Unfortunately, the favourite fell at the first fence. Ouch!

Oil wells are one sure way of getting rich – or are they? In 1982 the oil industry paid a staggering $1.6 billion for leases to drill in the Beaufort Sea, north of Alaska, 60 miles away from the hugely rich Prudhoe Bay oil field. The main investment was made by B.P. There were endless problems: a rare species of whale had to be protected, a road had to be built over the ice, and a million tons of gravel had to be shipped out to make an artificial island. Another $100 million had to be spent before drilling could begin but B.P. were optimistic. They hoped to find 5 billion barrels of oil when the drilling finally began in 1983. Instead they found water – lots of it – above and below ground. Could this have been the most expensive hole ever dug?

———— • ————

We all know about Mr Leeson and the fall of Barings but something similar had happened in 1973. Marc Columbo, a Swiss currency dealer who worked for the Midland Bank, was offered a job with Lloyds Bank International at their small branch in the Swiss town of Lugano on the Italian border.

Columbo did so well and made so much money for the bank he was soon made head of the foreign exchange operation at the branch. In 1973 the Egyptians launched their attack on Israel – the Yom Kippur War. Columbo took the view that the dollar would weaken as a result of the war. He sold $34 million on the 'forward' market. In other words he hoped to buy dollars at a lower price than he had promised to sell them at and make a good profit.

Unfortunately, the oil and energy crisis broke, driving the dollar up. Columbo had to buy his dollars at a far higher price than he was selling them at and made a massive loss.

To recover himself, and believing the dollar would continue to rise, he bought $100 million and paid for them in German marks and Swiss francs but now the dollar began to slide. He hurriedly tried to retrieve the situation by selling the extraordinary sum of $592 million forward but once again he got it wrong and the dollar rose steadily in value.

By the time Lloyds in London had picked up what was happening in their small Lugano branch and had suspended Columbo they had lost £33 million. There was never any suggestion that Columbo was dealing for personal profit. As he said later: 'For every dealer you need at least four administrators to check what he is doing. They do things that no ordinary banker understands.'

Twenty years later his words would be forgotten and the cost would be considerably higher.

———— • ————

In the 1930s when it was believed, 'the [German] bomber would always get through' and destroy England's towns and cities, Auberon Herbert, who owned Pixton in Somerset, designed the park in front of the house in the shape of the Union Jack. This was in response to the vandalism of his neighbour, Otto Gardiner, a member of the Cliveden Set. That gentleman cut his superb eighteenth-century deer park into the shape of a swastika in the hope that the Luftwaffe would not bomb his house!

———— • ————

An Actor's Lot is Not Always a Happy One

There are of course thousands of 'actors'' stories –
about misfortunes and disasters. I suppose that is
why 'live' theatre is so exciting. The audience
knows that that particular performance is unique
and, of course, they may, deep down be hoping
something will go wrong. I have had my fair share
of bad moments but nothing to match the experi-
ences of the nineteenth-century actor, Ronald
Coates. He was such a bad actor that on one occasion the audience tried to lynch him after a performance. He had to bribe managers to give him roles
and fellow actors are known to have demanded
police protection before going on stage with him,
but more often than not he was so bad the audience just laughed at him.

An Actor's Lot is Not
Always a Happy One

A lot of actors are really very shy – some are not! The actress Drew Barrymore wrote her autobiography when she was only 14 years old. But when we do get things wrong it all happens in public.

———— • ————

Robert Newton, for example – a celebrated drunk – was playing in *Richard II* with another actor who could sink a few pints: Wilfred Lawson. After a particularly liquid lunch they remembered there was a matinée that day. Half dressed, hair on end, Lawson struggled onto the stage. Blearily, he looked at the audience scattered thinly in the cavernous theatre and said: 'If you think I'm pissed, wait till you see the Duke of York!'

———— • ————

Even worse perhaps, were the Cherry Sisters who, in 1896, had a show on Broadway. They netted $200,000, which wasn't bad, but they had to perform behind a wire screen. Their performance was so awful the audience delighted at throwing things at them!

———— • ————

Donald Sinden has a good story of a Stratford production of *The Tempest* where everything that could go wrong did. When Prospero said to Ariel, 'Then to the elements be free', Ariel was supposed to take a few steps, wipe away a tear and fly off. On this occasion he took off all right but then hit the scenery with a resounding thwack before swinging back and knocking Prospero out cold!

*"They get worse. They now need a screen
for rehearsals as well."*

Sir Peter Ustinov tells many splendid stories of theatrical absurdities. One of his best, concerns that formidable *grande dame* of the English stage, Edith Evans. It was 1943 and Peter was directing *The Rivals* with Edith Evans playing Mrs Malaprop. As a bonus, the production boasted a section of the Berlin Philharmonic under their leader, Lance-Corporal Professor Doctor Reinhard Strietzel, all doing their bit against Hitler.

Peter writes: 'One of the drawbacks of the theatre was that there was no method of concealing the orchestra. Its members sat on the same level as the audience. It was merely the actors who were elevated. I noticed on the first night that the orchestra made use of a miniature chessboard in order to while away the time during the histrionics and often musicians crept forward like troops in a dugout to make a move.

'I hoped and prayed that Edith Evans would not notice what was going on but on the fourth night, during a brilliant tirade, she stopped dead. One eye had alighted on the tiny chessboard just as the viola player had spotted a crack in the enemy defence and was creeping forward to deliver the *coup de grâce*.

'She was livid, and after the show I accosted Professor Strietzel. To soften the blow I told him he had never played better than on that night.

'His face lit up. "You are a *real* musician," he counter-flattered.

'"There's only one thing . . . one criticism."

'"Ach!" His face darkened.

'"The game of chess. It's frightfully distracting."

'"It *distracts* you? No! You are too fine an artist to be distracted. It's zis voman!"

'The next night Edith found it hard to concentrate. As soon as I came on stage I saw what was happening. The orchestra, deprived of its chessboard, had now arranged the lights on its music-stands so that its members were lit from beneath, and they all followed Edith's every move looking like war criminals following the arguments of their advocate with misgivings and resignation.

'Once again, at the end of the performance, I was compelled to accost Professor Strietzel.

'"Why do you follow Edith Evans with your eyes in a manner to disturb any performer, any artist?"

'"First it vas the chessboard. Correct me if I am wrong. Chess ve shouldn't play . . ."

'"That is correct."

'"So ve leave the chessboard at home. Vot else can ve do? Ve follow the play. Ve look at the voman."

'Suddenly the constriction of his voice and the coolness of presentation of the facts deserted him. He shouted: "You think it gives us *pleasure* to vatch zis voman? Ve who have seen Paula Wessley at her height."'

———— • ————

An Actor's Lot is Not
Always a Happy One

For any actor Noël Coward is the wittiest commentator on our peculiar profession and I make no excuse for repeating two or three of his best *bon mots*. His 'put downs' make me want to say: 'I wish I'd said that!'

Rehearsing one of his plays, Coward was irritated by a young actor in a small part who kept on asking about 'the motivation' of his character. 'In your case,' Coward informed him sharply, 'it's your pay packet.'

———— • ————

During a rehearsal of *Blithe Spirit* the actress, Claudette Colbert, got so furious with Coward she shouted at him: 'If you're not careful, I'll throw something at you!'
Coward snapped back: 'Well, you might begin with my cues!'

One theatre critic Coward particularly disliked and who had been very rude about Coward's plays came backstage to praise his performance in a play in which he was starring called *The Second Man* by S.N. Behrman. The critic infuriated Coward by commenting: 'I always said you could act better than you could write.'

'And I've always said the same about you,' was Coward's withering response.

———— • ————

Another journalist went up to Coward and said: 'Have you anything to say to the *Star* ?'

'Of course,' Coward replied, 'twinkle.'

———— • ————

As he said on another occasion: 'My reputation's terrible which comforts me a lot.'

And finally, a splendid story Sir Dirk Bogarde tells sums up the perils of overacting. When Bogarde was a struggling young actor at the beginning of the war, he was delighted to get some quite good notices in a small part in a J.B. Priestley play called *Cornelius*. The next night he really set out to slay them, throwing his arms about and overacting wildly. At last, Max Adrian, in the role of a timid clerk, got so irritated he slammed a heavy accounts book down on Bogarde's head knocking him out cold. 'Never do that again!' Max Adrian exclaimed. The audience rocked with laughter thinking it all part of the play.

———— • ————

Spooky Showers

I have always relished strange tales of
inexplicable 'happenings' – especially when
highly respectable people experience . . .
well, listen to this!

Mr Roland Moody of Southampton was working in
his greenhouse when he witnessed one of the
strangest meteorological malfunctions. It was
February 1978. He was pricking out his seedlings
when:

'I heard this whooshing sound on the glass above
me. I didn't take a lot of notice of it but about
three quarters of an hour later I heard it again. I
looked up and found the glass above me covered in
what we discovered afterwards to be mustard and

cress seed. But the most peculiar thing about it was that the cress seed was covered in jelly. In fact, if you were to put your finger down on the seed to pick it up, it stuck to your fingers and you couldn't get rid of it. And this shower was repeated five or six times in the course of the day. Each time more and more of this mustard and cress came down until it covered the whole garden. It was most peculiar because we then started treading it indoors on our feet and there you could smell the mustard and cress without a shadow of doubt.'

In the weeks that followed, Mr and Mrs Moody and their neighbours suffered showers of other seeds and vegetables including beans and peas.

One of the neighbours complained: 'Every time I opened the door I was showered with broad beans.'

Apparently, this is no isolated case. Many people have been showered in vegetable matter including Mr and Mrs Osborne of Bristol who were showered with hazelnuts when passing a Peugeot car sales-room. 'There was a click as if I had lost a button and then I realized it was not a button I had lost but something that had fallen from the sky.' The surprised couple found they were being 'drenched' in . . . hazelnuts. And what was most peculiar was that hazelnuts weren't even in season!

Herrings, squid, lizards and frogs are just some of the many reported 'showers'. Here is one from 1829. Lord Eastnor wrote:

'Soon after a most violent storm of rain and wind, three small crabs weighing from one-and-a-quarter to one-and-three-quarter ounces were found in the area of the workhouse at Reigate and a fourth was afterwards found at a little distance, I think the following morning . . . '

———— • ————

In 1918 another 'fishy' shower was reported: three-inch sand eels fell in Sunderland. Much more frightening and, don't forget, this was long before aeroplanes could be blamed for things falling out of the sky, in 1848 in Scotland, a ball of ice, 20-feet round, narrowly missed falling through the roof of a farm house. It was composed of diamond-shaped ice-blocks but there was no sign of hail or snow storms anywhere in the district.

No one has ever found a satisfactory solution for why people have been 'showered' by strange objects and if they did I'd insist on saying, **'I don't believe it!'**, for who wants these mysteries explained? I don't for one!

———— • ————

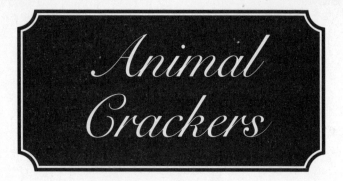

Are animals crackers or are they saner than we are? I have gathered all the evidence so you can judge for yourself!

———— • ————

In France, it's widely believed that if a bachelor steps on a cat's tail he won't find a wife for at least another year.

In America, in May 1963, a cow called Fawn was swept into the air by a tornado and travelled half a mile before landing safely in another farmer's field. Five years later she was swept up in another tornado. Flying over a bus, she was spotted by a group of tourists landing again without hurting herself. She died at the ripe old age of 25.

———— • ————

Kangaroos are only an inch long at birth.

———— • ————

A chameleon's body is half as long as its tongue.

In the Middle Ages, animals were sometimes tried in a full court of law for crimes such as exerting an evil influence on a human being. If found guilty they were sentenced to death. In the eleventh century St Bernard excommunicated a swarm of bees for buzzing too loudly while he was preaching.

———— • ————

More recently, a New Zealand cow was sentenced to two days in jail for eating the grass in front of the city courthouse.

———— • ————

The world's largest bee, the carpenter, has tried to mate with everything that flies including birds, light aircraft and hang gliders.

"That was a mistake, putting her on the top bunk."

The Romans cured toothache by tying toads to their jaws.

———— • ————

The owner of Langan's Brasserie in London once scuttled across the floor on all fours and bit the hind leg of a small dog.

———— • ————

Goldfish remember better in cold water than in warm water.

A Canadian man was so incensed by having his pilot's licence revoked that he bombed Calgary with hundreds of pounds of pig manure.

———— • ————

Did you know that crickets hear through their knees, cicadas through their stomachs and snakes through their tongues?

———— • ————

An Alsatian dog was arrested in Seville in 1983 for snatching handbags in the city centre.

According to a study carried out in California in 1966, pigs are the only mammals other than man that are capable of getting sunburned.

———— • ————

Bulls don't see red – they are colour-blind.

———— • ————

Percy Bysshe Shelley hated cats so much that he once tied a kite to a cat's tail in a thunderstorm in the hope that the cat would be electrocuted. I am glad to say lightning struck neither cat nor poet.

*"There's no profit in pigs anymore.
The sun cream is so expensive."*

The black widow spider eats its mate after mating. It can eat up to 26 'husbands' a day.

———— • ————

Snails can sleep for three years at a go and they only mate once in a lifetime . . . but it can last for up to 12 hours.

———— • ————

Hummingbirds can't walk.

An albatross can stay airborne for days on end without flapping its wings.

———— • ————

Dead jellyfish can sting and octopuses can eat themselves if they get very upset.

———— • ————

Polar bears can smell you up to 20 miles away.

I Don't Believe It!

Electric eels can produce 400 volts of electricity.

———— • ————

Only male canaries sing.

———— • ————

Fully-grown whales eat three tons of food a day.

———— • ————

Camels' humps store fat not water.

Dolphins sleep with one eye open.

———— • ————

Chameleons can look in different directions at once.

———— • ————

In Ancient Egypt, when cats died – they were sacred animals – their owners would shave their eyebrows in mourning.

Yes, I guess the case is proved: it's humans who are crackers.

Appalling Poetry

There are many claims for the honour of being the worst published poet. Sir Alfred Austin is one candidate and he was made Poet Laureate in 1896.

Someone once chided him for the grammatical errors in his verse. He excused himself by saying: 'I dare not alter these things; they come to me from above.' The trouble is that his two best/worst lines, on the illness of the Prince of Wales, may not have been written by him at all but by someone sending him up:

Across the wires the electric message came:
"He is no better, he is much the same."

The prize has to go to a favourite 'poet' of mine: William McGonagall whose epics include his poetic account of the Tay Bridge Disaster of 1879. However his 'Address to the Rev George Gilfillan' may be his best – or is it worst – poem. In part it reads:

———— • ————

All hail to the Rev George Gilfillan of Dundee,
He is the greatest preacher I did ever hear or see.
He is a man of genius bright,
And in him his congregation does delight,
Because they find him to be honest and plain,
Affable in temper, and seldom known to complain.
He preaches in a plain straightforward way,
The people flock to hear him night and day,
And hundreds from the doors are often turned away,
Because he is the greatest preacher of the present day.

All right, I confess! I don't think he's *that* bad. What do you think?

I DON'T BELIEVE IT!

It is not always easy to be right when making judgements about works of art, particularly music. Tchaikovsky thought Brahms was 'a fraud and a scoundrel'. But he in turn was dismissed by the nineteenth-century music critic James Davison. He called Tchaikovsky's *Romeo and Juliet* 'rubbish'. He hated all Wagner's music and called Schubert 'beneath criticism'. Berlioz was a 'lunatic' and Verdi's *Rigoletto* 'would flicker and flare for a night or two and then be forgotten.'

A lot of people don't realize that the title of *One Foot in the Grave* is ironic. Victor may have one foot in the said grave but the other is well and truly out and he intends to keep it out! Talking of graves however, there are many ways of making sure you are not easily forgotten. Lyndon Colegrave of Kinderhook, Illinois was a golf fanatic. So it's no surprise that his gravestone provides him with a huge golf ball on a tee complete with golf clubs ready for use on those heavenly greens!

———— • ————

In the 1840s, the tenth duke of Hamilton spent the huge sum of £11,000 buying an Ancient Egyptian sarcophagus in which to be interred. Unfortunately when he died in 1852, the Duke proved to be too long for the sarcophagus and, before he could be buried, his legs had to be cut off.

When Ray Tse was killed in a car crash in 1980, his brother gave him the gravestone he would have wanted: a stone replica of his Mercedes-Benz 18-foot-long. Talking of cars . . . Sandra West of San Antonio, Texas, who died in 1977 was buried in her beloved blue Ferrari. She took the precaution of having it encased in concrete to deter ghoulish grave robbers.

———— • ————

And finally . . . fame can disturb even eternal rest: James Dean, the film star was buried under pink granite in Fairmount, Indiana. The headstone was stolen in 1983. It was found four years later dumped behind the Fire Station at Fort Wayne, 50 miles away!

I don't believe It!

Probably, like me, most of you don't believe
in fairies, however there are some people
who swear they have seen 'the little people'.

———— • ————

Mary Tredgold, a children's author saw a fairy on
Mull:
'My bus drew into a lay-by and I looked idly at an
expanse of peat outside the window. This tiny
young man was standing beside a tallish clump of
heather with his foot on a spade. He was wearing
blue dungarees and a very white shirt . . .'
He was just 18-inches high!

I Don't Believe It!

You don't believe it? Well, what about the boy who was bathing with friends in the river Moy at Foxford, County Mayo? On a hot summer's day at the beginning of the century he saw a little man only four-feet tall dodge behind a boulder. He was wearing a collarless black coat buttoned up to his chin. He had a flat face and whiskers and wore . . . a large grin.

———— • ————

Maybe there are more fairies in Ireland than anywhere else. In 1951, a little man dressed in black was seen by two girls walking along a road in County Wicklow. He was two to three-feet tall and was dressed in black . . .

———— • ————

In 1959, John Byrne was moving a large bush with a bulldozer when a three-foot-tall man ran out from under it. Where the bush had been, there was a great flagstone which no one could ever move . . .

You still say: **'I don't believe it!'**? Oh well, here's one last sighting!

Violet Tweedale was walking in Devon in 1915; on a wild iris, she saw:
'. . . a tiny green man. He was five-inches long . . . with a merry face and something red in the form of a cap on his head. For a full minute he remained in view. Then he vanished.'

So there you are . . . say after me . . . 'I believe in fairies'!

Two Feet in the Grave

I owe a great deal to David Renwick who, in *One Foot in the Grave*, gave me the wonderfully comic and curmudgeonly Victor Meldrew to play. Death is often funny, absurd, ridiculous when it is not tragic. Indeed, I think we should laugh at it more...

———— • ————

An Italian woman who wanted to commit suicide by gassing herself, closed all the windows in her apartment, turned on her oven and then proceeded to light a last cigarette. She blew up her building killing two other tenants, but she survived!

When the French writer, Victor Hugo, died, Parisian prostitutes wore black scarves round their private parts in respectful tribute to one of their most illustrious clients. (I have to say, I can't quite see how these scarves were draped!) The Government even gave them a grant so they wouldn't suffer a loss of income if they knocked off work early to attend the funeral.

———— • ————

In 1986 an 18-stone man tried to hang himself from an aqueduct over the River Ouse. He drowned when the rope broke.

———— • ————

In 1938 a woman called Phyllis Newcombe spontaneously combusted while dancing a waltz in a public dance hall.

A Parisian grocer was jailed for two years in 1978 for stabbing his wife with a wedge of hard cheese.

———— • ————

An American newsreader called Christine Chubbock shot herself in front of the television cameras some years ago. When her notes were checked they revealed she had actually allowed time in the schedule for her death so that other programmes would not start late.

———— • ————

King Henry I, who fathered at least 21 illegitimate children, died of a 'surfeit of lampreys'.

"How much do you want?"

I Don't Believe It!

In Texas, when Orvell Lloyd was asked why he had killed his mother-in-law, he said he had mistaken her for a racoon. Yes, you're right: **'I don't believe it!'**

———— • ————

A husband who strangled his wife because she kept on waking him in the night to ask him to help her with the crossword was acquitted on the grounds of temporary insanity.

———— • ————

When French police charged Louis Pilar with shooting his wife he blamed a three-week TV strike: 'There was nothing to look at. I was bored,' he said.

Paul Hubert was 21 years into a life sentence before it was realized he had been convicted of murdering . . . himself.

———— • ————

In Brazil, a 107-year-old man called Pedro de Silva was sentenced to six years in prison after hiring hit men to kill his son-in-law. The Prosecution asked for a long sentence as Pedro was in such good health.

———— • ————

The great actress Sarah Bernhardt, (who played Juliet in *Romeo and Juliet* at the age of 70) had an obsession with death and enjoyed visiting dissecting rooms where she used to poke the corpses with her parasol. She liked to take her coffin with her when she went on tour and sometimes slept in it.

Another great lady obsessed with death was Florence Nightingale. Like Joan of Arc, she heard 'voices' and when touring hospital wards she carried a pet owl in her pocket. In 1857 she became so convinced she was going to die that she made all her own funeral arrangements. She lived for a further 53 years, the last 40 spent in bed.

———— • ————

Talking of dissecting rooms, in 1890 a Swedish man desperate for money sold his body to a medical academy for dissection after his death. Twenty years later he tried to buy it back but the doctors refused to sell. He sued but lost his case. Not only that – he had to pay them damages for having had two teeth extracted without their permission.

Poor Iris Somerville was killed in 1982 in London when lightning struck the metal support in her brassiere.

———— • ————

Let's end with a quotation from the great American lawyer, Clarence Darrow: 'I have never killed a man but I have read many obituaries with a lot of pleasure!'

The Law's an Ass

I'm pleased to say I've never had much to do with lawyers. I did play one – Jeremy Parsons QC in *Crown Court* and I hope that that is the closest I get to appearing in one of those terrifying buildings. There's no doubt however that when the law is not very frightening it can be an ass! One rather unusual judicial decision occurred in New Mexico in 1982 when a 27-year-old woman was convicted of shooting her husband in a domestic dispute. The judge sentenced her to three years in college on the grounds that, since she had previously qualified for a scholarship that very year, it would be cheaper for the state to have her at university than in jail! Here are some more cases that prove the law is an ass.

In Minnesota it's illegal to hang men and women's undergarments on the same line.

In February 1978, an Iowa judge dismissed a drink-driving charge against a man he ruled to have been too drunk to have consented to the blood alcohol test that proved he was inebriated.

——— • ———

In 1983 magistrates rejected an application for a sports and social club because the building was deemed to be a fire hazard. The applicants were . . . the local fire brigade.

——— • ———

Nebraska once had a law making it illegal to teach foreign languages to young children. In Massachusetts, in 1784, a law was passed whereby unmarried couples living together could be brought to the gallows and given 39 lashes with ropes around their necks.

From 1300 to 1500 it was illegal for Englishmen to eat three meals a day. In ancient China the stealing of a Pekinese dog – which was held sacred – was punishable by death, as was smoking in Czarist Russia. In the reign of Queen Elizabeth I, a law was passed making men with beards pay a levy.

———— • ————

From 1659 to 1681 it was illegal to celebrate Christmas in Massachusetts. In Indiana there was once a law prohibiting people from travelling on buses within four hours of eating garlic. Cutting down trees was technically a hanging offence in Britain until 1819.

———— • ————

To this day it's illegal to have a nude dummy on display in New York, and in Arizona, it's illegal to hunt camels. And if you live in California you can't buy a mousetrap without first getting a hunting licence!

———— • ————

However, on a happier note, in 1975, David Philips, a 77-year-old man from Cardiff was fined £5 for 42 kiss-and-run incidents involving female traffic wardens.

———— • ————

Of course drunkenness cannot be tolerated: in Brisbane the police arrested a man for being drunk in charge of a wheelchair, while in Norway, in 1980, a man was fined for being drunk in charge of a mobile vacuum cleaner.

A couple of years earlier the pilot of a light air-craft, running out of fuel, had to make an emergency landing on a toll road in Illinois. He promptly received a ticket for, 'entering at the wrong junction' and for failing to pay 30 cents toll.

———— • ————

Parking fines seem almost as inevitable as taxes. In one Swedish town the fire brigade received a bill for £100 for parking illegally while putting out a fire. Something similar happened in Swindon in 1985 when an ambulance attending an emergency call was fined for 'illegal standing'.

———— • ————

"Surely one of you has change for the meter?"

I Don't Believe It!

In Leeds, a man was let off a charge of drunkenness even though it was his 500th appearance in court. Two days later he was in court again on the usual charge; his excuse? 'I was celebrating my 500th appearance in court!' As Dean Martin said: 'You're not drunk if you can lie on the floor without holding on.'

———— • ————

In Dallas, some years ago, an undercover policeman began to chat up a lady of the night in a dimly lit alleyway with the intention of slapping an injunction on her for soliciting. Before he could make his move, she slipped the handcuffs on him! He hadn't bargained for the fact that she might be an undercover cop too.

Did you know that duelling is quite legal in Paraguay – so long as both parties are regular blood donors? Or that in New York there's an old law which has never been repealed that prohibits women from smoking in public?

———— • ————

And then there's the Florida man who claimed against his insurance company for injuries caused when the pavement collapsed. His claim was dismissed on the grounds that this was an Act of God, so he did what any reasonable man would do in the circumstances – he sued God. The latter did not appear but a local priest gave evidence on His behalf. If the case goes against God he may have a problem if he wants to appeal to a higher court!

I Don't Believe It!

The police have their problems too. For instance, the house of a Venezuelan criminal straddles the border with Colombia. When the police try to arrest him he hides in his bedroom until they go away. You see, the bedroom is in Colombia, a country in which he has no criminal record.

I'm always on the lookout for bizarre notices, but I've never come across anything better than these! In 1978, outside Epsom District Hospital, there was a notice that said: **Guard dogs operating.** I knew the National Health Service was short of money but there has to be a limit to what patients have to put up with. Here is a list of the 'nutty notices' I have really enjoyed compiling:

———— • ————

In a furniture shop:
We stand behind every bed we sell.

I Don't Believe It!

In a grocers:
Please don't handle the fruit. Ask for Debbie.

——— • ———

In a bakery:
Ladies get fresh in here.

——— • ———

In a video shop:
Why not rent out a movie for a dull evening?

In a bargain basement:
Don't go to another shop to be cheated – come in here.

———— • ————

In a cinema showing *The Ten Commandments* :
Thou shalt not smoke.

———— • ————

In a hotel:
All the fire extinguishers must be examined at least ten days before any fire.

I Don't Believe It!

In a drapery shop:
Gents' trousers slashed.

———— • ————

In another hotel:
Customers should note that any complaints about rudeness in the staff will be dealt with very severely.

———— • ————

In a boarding-house:
Please do not turn on TV except in use.

In a golf club:
**Life Membership. Apply Now.
Offer for limited period only.**

"I think I preferred the smaller slash."

Oddballs

The great thing about being an actor is that
you get a chance for a short time to play
extraordinary people – some, to say the least
of it, eccentric – like Dr Rance who I played
in the Royal National Theatre production of
What the Butler Saw by Joe Orton.
However, I can't pretend even Dr Rance is
in the same class as these nut cases:

———— • ————

On his return to England after visiting India,
Lytton Strachey, the writer, kept all the clocks at
Calcutta time.

ODDBALLS

In 1969, having already eaten 22,500 razor blades and a ton of glass, a Yugoslav man set about his greatest gastronomic challenge: a bus.
And there's the Russian, Sergei Kelnikov, who holds the world record in pig-kissing. (The imagination boggles!)

———— • ————

Simeon Stylites lived for 30 years on top of a 60-foot column in the desert. Sometimes he stood erect with his arms outstretched in the form of a cross but generally he lay on his back bringing his head forward at intervals to meet his knees. All the time he recited the rosary.

———— • ————

Emma Smith had herself buried in a coffin for a 101 days. She had food and drink piped down to her and communicated with her friends via closed-circuit TV.

———— • ————

Deborah Brown and her husband Robert, fans of the Texas Longhorns football team, were determined to have their second child born on Texas soil – despite the fact that they were living in California. They licked the problem by arranging to have a sack of Texas dirt brought up from Dallas and placed in a sterile bag under the delivery table.

———— • ————

Majorcan waiter Paco Vila had a problem: he was too skinny so none of the girls would dance with him. To get round this problem, before he went to a disco he would put on several jumpers to make himself look burly. It worked! The trouble was he danced so much he lost even more weight sweating under all those clothes. Paco's story ended when one evening he collapsed with heat-stroke while boogeying with a blonde. Doctors had to remove a jacket and nine jumpers before they could treat him.

—— • ——

Gene and Lynda Ballard opted for a rather unusual divorce in 1986 – skydiving at 120 miles per hour above California. Lynda's lawyer followed them out of the aircraft and served divorce papers on Gene at 12,000 feet. Then, after a final mid-air kiss, they drifted apart . . . literally!

*"You should have decided beforehand
who got custody of the parachute."*

Even republicans would have to admit to being fascinated by royalty – the intrigues and scandals as well as the pomp and ceremony. Many people even *dream* about having tea with the Queen. One thing is certain, royals have more opportunity than most of us for being absurd. We won't go into toe-sucking and the activities of our own dear royals but here are one or two facts about some other royals.

———— • ————

King George IV hated his wife, Caroline of Brunswick. When he was brought news of Napoleon's death, the messenger was not precise enough: 'Your Majesty, your greatest enemy is dead!' he announced. The King replied 'Is she by God?'

As he neared death, George IV drank gallons of cherry brandy and suffered delusions of having fought and won the battle of Waterloo. His doctor, Sir William Knighton, advised: 'His Majesty has only to leave off cherry brandy and, rest assured, he will gain no more victories.'

———— • ————

The French Bourbon kings were also famous for their gluttony and drunkenness. Louis XIV ate so much, even into his eighties, people thought he had a tapeworm inside him. Louis XVIII was an equally obsessive eater but died thin on account of the dropsy. Louis XVI was known affectionately as 'the fat pig' because he ate so much. (Since he only took two baths in his lifetime he was rather smelly too.) He did not consummate his marriage with Marie Antoinette for seven years owing to over-grown foreskin on his penis. He was at last persuaded to have surgery and lost his virginity on his twenty-third birthday.

The Kaiser, William II, was by any standards a disaster. Not only did he lead Germany into the First World War but he also thoroughly disliked his wife Augusta and couldn't even be bothered to tell her he had been made Emperor. He fancied himself a naval leader and actually designed a warship. He sent his design to the great naval architect, Admiral Brin. Brin finally reported back to the Emperor: If built the ship would outgun anything else on the high seas, he began tactfully. Its range and speed was excellent, its internal design was a miracle of ingenuity. The only problem was, the report concluded, if it were actually put in the water it would sink like a stone.

———— • ————

Kings are as gullible as the rest of us. Louis XIV for instance fell for this really admirable con trick. He was told that an ambassador from the Shah of Persia had arrived at the French court and craved an audience with the King. King Louis put up the ambassador in a luxurious suite in the palace and sent Cardinal Richelieu to say that the King would receive the ambassador in the famous Gallery of Mirrors. There was a great ball and banquet and the King presented the ambassador with a portrait of himself framed in diamonds and gifts worth many millions of francs and was given in return a small bag of jewels.

The ambassador sorrowfully announced that this was all he was able to present the King with as his master's rich gifts were still on the high seas.

A few days later the ambassador sent word that at last his master's treasure had arrived. The King waited eagerly for the ambassador to present himself at court. Unfortunately the ambassador never arrived. He had vanished along with all the wealth with which he had been presented. At least, the King thought, he had the bag of jewels but on close inspection these turned out to be coloured glass.

Despite a search, the 'ambassador' was never discovered.

Leopold II of the Belgians took his second wife from a Paris brothel. He was 74, she was 16. Once, when he was with his ministers and his nephew and heir apparent, the wind blew some papers onto the floor. 'You pick them up', he ordered his nephew. When his ministers looked embarrassed to see the prince humiliated, he added: 'A constitutional monarch must learn to stoop.'

———— • ————

I said there'd be a lot of lists: here's one
– some facts and figures I found difficult
to credit.

Only six people died in the Great Fire of London
in 1666.

———— • ————

Buzz Aldrin said: 'Neil Armstrong was the first
man to walk on the moon. I am the first man to
piss his pants on the moon!'

The number of possible bridge hands is over 635,000 million, which means that the likelihood of being dealt the same hand twice is only once every 72 million years.

———— • ————

The philosopher John Stuart Mill could read Greek fluently at the age of three.

———— • ————

In the court of King Henry VIII knitting was a male pursuit.

I Don't Believe It!

People are a quarter of an inch smaller walking than in bed because the vertebrae are squashed when the body is vertical.

———— • ————

A frog's tongue grows from *the front* of its mouth.

———— • ————

Ho Chi Minh once worked as a dishwasher in the Carlton Hotel in London.

Saturn's density is so low that, if it fell into a vast area of water, it would float.

——— • ———

Niagara Falls is switched off at night.

——— • ———

Modern binoculars are more powerful than Galileo's telescope.

Pope John XXIII liked to sit in his penthouse flat in the Vatican and watch through his binoculars people hanging out their washing on the flat roofs of their houses.

———— • ————

Pope John Paul II delivered his 1982 Christmas blessing in 42 languages.

———— • ————

Peter Arbuez, who was responsible for the deaths of over 40,000 people during the Spanish Inquisition, was canonized in 1860.

More people are kicked to death by donkeys than are killed in air crashes and the odds against being attacked by a shark are 30 million to one.

———— • ————

William Tell couldn't have shot an apple from his son's head with a crossbow because crossbows were unknown in Switzerland in the thirteenth century.

———— • ————

On a clear night, over 2000 stars are visible to the naked eye.

One in every thousand Americans is a murderer and there are, on average, 16 murders a day in New York. Perhaps this explains the result of a world-wide medical study which found that Americans suffer more from headaches than any other nationality.

———— • ————

Although there are more women than men in the world, the men weigh 15 per cent more. Women can talk longer than men with less effort because their vocal chords are shorter and they need less breath to make sound carry. Women get drunk faster than men. Their bodies are 58 per cent water, whereas men's are 70 per cent, which dilutes the alcohol more.

I Don't Believe It!

An American was granted a divorce in Maine on the grounds that his wife made him live on a diet of pea soup and nothing else.

———— • ————

Greta Garbo worked as a manicurist in Sweden before she became a film star.

———— • ————

Domestic life is bliss – or is it? Apparently the first four minutes at the breakfast table and the first four minutes after arriving home are the flash points of three quarters of all marital disputes. Women tend to kill their husbands in the kitchen while men kill their wives in the bedroom.

——— • ———

Eugene Schneider objected when a divorce court judge in New Jersey ordered him to divide his property equally with his wife. When the judge insisted his order be carried out, Schneider took his chain saw and cut his $80,000 wooden bungalow in half.

I DON'T BELIEVE IT!

New Yorker Zaza Kimmont saw red when she walked into her bathroom and noticed a strange toothbrush next to her husband's and traces of lipstick on the bristles. She threw everything breakable at the wall doing over $10,000 worth of damage – only to find that while she had been away her mother-in-law had been to stay and left her toothbrush behind!

———— • ————

Everything happens in New York! A New York father wanted to be a good *mother*. He breast-fed his baby daughter for three months with the aid of female sex-hormone tablets.

"Yes but surely he's not still breast-feeding him?"

But I must not give the impression that all marriages are unhappy – far from it! Richard Wagner's wife, Cosima, was so distraught when her husband died that she clung to his corpse for 24 hours.

——— • ———

And recently, a man named Walter Davis went to a computer dating service to find himself a new wife. After going through its memory banks the computer came up with a girl called Ethel Davis – his former wife. He didn't argue with technology . . . and remarried her! (Computer dating seems to work better than 'lonely hearts' advertisements in newspapers. A 22-year-old Los Angeles man advertised for someone to accompany him on a vacation to South America. He got one reply – from his widowed mother!)

Have you ever considered the variety of
ways in which folk have shuffled off this
mortal coil? Try these for size!

The Greek painter Zeuxis laughed so hard at one of
his own paintings he broke a blood vessel and died.

———— • ————

Claudius, the Emperor of Rome, choked to death
on a feather.

Allan Pinkerton, the founder of the detective agency, stumbled during his morning walk, bit his tongue and died of gangrene.

———— • ————

In the seventeenth and eighteenth centuries the main thing necessary to avoid dying in agony was to make sure *no* doctors were in attendance. We now all know about the madness of King George III thanks to Alan Bennett's marvellous play but what about King Charles II? At his deathbed – at least it turned out to be his deathbed – he was attended by no less than 14 doctors. They bled pints of blood from him, made him vomit and open his bowels. They fed him gall stones and essence of a dead-man's skull. A true gentleman – he merely asked to be forgiven for taking 'a most unconscionable time dying'!

Arnold Bennett, the novelist, died in Paris of typhoid contracted from a glass of water he drank to prove that Parisian water was safe to drink.

———— • ————

Exotic dancer Isadora Duncan was strangled to death when her long scarf became entangled in the wheel of a motorcar.

———— • ————

The French composer Jean Baptiste Lully met his maker as a result of his habit of pounding the floor with a large pointed cane as he conducted. One day, he accidentally struck his foot with the cane so violently that he got blood poisoning and died.

In 1986 an Indonesian MP had just succeeded in getting a new hearse for his local hospital when he was killed in a road accident. He became the hearse's first passenger.

———— • ————

In 1981 German newspapers reported that a woman believed she could stimulate her rather somnolent husband by frightening him. One day, when she heard him come in the front door, she hid in a cupboard and jumped out at him screaming. Unfortunately he was so scared he ran away, tripped on a carpet and plunged to his death from an upstairs window.

The Chinese poet Li Po died when, on a boat one night, he leant over the side to kiss the reflection of the moon on the water and fell in and drowned.

———— • ————

Roman consul Fabius choked to death on a single goat hair in the milk he was drinking.

———— • ————

Pope Hadrian IV died when a fly stuck in his throat as he was drinking water from a fountain.

I Don't Believe It!

The Greek playwright Aeschylus was killed when an eagle dropped a tortoise on his head.

———— • ————

Before John Farmer died, he left instructions that broken glass was to be scattered round his feet in his mausoleum. Why? 'Because otherwise the worms would eat me, the ducks would eat the worms and my family would eat the ducks. And I don't want to be eaten by my relatives.'

———— • ————

Attila the Hun is alleged to have died of a burst blood vessel when he got too excited by a virgin. Apparently, he came and went, so to speak.

"You were lucky you got the terrapin."

Tsar Paul I of Russia decreed that anyone who mentioned his baldness – a point on which he was sensitive – would be flogged to death.

———— • ————

King Gustav of Sweden was so convinced that coffee was dangerous he sentenced a criminal to drink himself to death with it. The 'execution' lasted until the man was 83.

———— • ————

Austrian, Hans Steininger, who had the longest beard in the world, tripped over it one day when he was climbing a staircase and fell to his death.

Harry Houdini, the escapologist, died when a student punched him in the stomach without warning. The student had heard that Houdini could take hard blows without pain but had not realized this was only after Houdini had tensed his muscles to prepare for the blow.

———— • ————

And one odd entrance: George of Epirus was born during the funeral of his mother. The pall bearers heard crying from the coffin and, when they opened it, he slipped out of the womb totally healthy.

It's so easy to point the finger at sports commentators and the verbal slips they make especially when broadcasting 'live' under extreme pressure. It's a tough job but still, here are a few of their 'best efforts' to enjoy:

Being naturally right-footed, Trevor doesn't often chance his arm with his left.

———— • ————

Souness gave Fleck a second chance and he grabbed it with both feet.

I don't think cricket should be used as a political football.

———— • ————

Every time he gets the ball he moves around like a banana-shaped umbrella to cut the pitch off.

———— • ————

That was a great goal by Moss – straight into the text book.

Obviously for Scunthorpe it would be a nice scalp to put Wimbledon on their bottoms.

———— • ————

I can't see us getting beat if we get our tails in front.

———— • ————

The ball slid away from his left boot, which was poised with the trigger cocked.

Stevens got to the line, crossed the ball and Lineker wrapped it all up with his head.

———— • ————

I owe a lot to my parents, especially my mum and dad.
(Greg Norman)

———— • ————

Rally points scoring is 20 points for the fastest, 18 points for the second fastest, right down to six points for the slowest fastest.
(Murray Walker)

I Don't Believe It!

We did nothing wrong in the match except lose it. (Kim Hughes)

———— • ————

Born in Italy, most of his fights have been in his native New York. (Des Lynam)

———— • ————

Alderman knows he's either going to get a wicket or he isn't. (Steve Brenkley)

His throw went absolutely nowhere near where it was going. (Richie Bennaud)

——— • ———

The boxer isn't doing what's expected from him – bleeding from the nose.
(Harry Carpenter)

——— • ———

The Kenyans haven't done much in the last two Olympic Games – in fact they haven't competed.
(Brendan Foster)

I Don't Believe It!

The American's heads are on their chins a little bit at the moment. (Ron Pickering)

———— • ————

The Republic of China are back in the Olympic Games for the first time.
(David Coleman)

———— • ————

It's obvious these Russian swimmers are determined to do well on American soil.
(Anita Lonsborough)

She's finally tasted the sweet smell of success.
(Ian Edwards)

———— • ————

Obviously, on paper it's a very good game. Do you think in theory it'll be one?
(Andrew Giddley)

———— • ————

He's running on his nerve ends.
(Peter West)

Britain's last gold medal was a bronze in 1952 in Helsinki.
(Nigel Smith)

———— • ————

He's 31 this year. Last year he was 30.
(David Coleman)

———— • ————

Zola Budd: so small you literally can't see her, but there she is.
(Alan Parry)

Satisfying Sex

Back to sex again and why not? As Mae West said: 'To err is human but it feels Divine!' (Sorry Hugh!) So here are some more unbelievable yet true facts about what, it is said, men think about once every four minutes. (According to Joan Rivers, the American writer and TV personality, 'The only time a woman really has an orgasm is when she's shopping – otherwise she's faking it.' But I don't believe it – I think?)

Peter the Great had his wife executed for infidelity, but he still loved her enough to have her head preserved in a jar.

After sex, the female marine bristleworm eats her partner's sex organ. (I've heard of oral sex but this is going too far!)

———— • ————

An exotic dancer named Mavisa Lonez was asked for a courtroom demonstration of her act. When she had finished the Ohio jury broke into spontaneous applause and slapped a fine for indecency on her.

———— • ————

One of the King of Tonga's duties used to be to deflower every virgin on his island. One king was still doing his duty at the age of 80.

MGM studios had the menstrual cycles of its actresses plotted on a wall chart so they could plan their movies round them.

———— • ————

Laura Bell, one of Victorian London's most famous prostitutes, eventually took up preaching and married a minister.

———— • ————

Sex came a poor 14th in a survey conducted some time ago on America's favourite leisure occupations – lower than house repairs and gardening.

"I thought she'd given up prostitution
when she started preaching."

I Don't Believe It!

In 1863, during the battle of Mississippi, a soldier was hit in the scrotum by a bullet which carried away his left testicle. The same bullet penetrated the abdomen of a 17-year-old girl in a nearby house. 278 days later the girl gave birth to a little boy. Three weeks later a doctor operated on the baby and removed the bullet from it. The doctor concluded the girl had been impregnated by the bullet passing through the man's testicle into the girl's ovary. When the doctor told the soldier of his findings, the soldier went to see the girl, got to know her, love her and eventually married her. They had three subsequent children in the normal way but none resembled the soldier as much as the first child.

I don't believe it!

———— • ————

In 1981, crowds of shoppers in a Montevideo market stared in astonishment as a middle-aged couple lay down behind the stalls and had sex in the gutter. A court later dismissed the charge of public indecency as their doctor had told them to introduce as much variety as possible into their love-making.

———— • ————

Painless childbirth was opposed by churchmen for a long time on the grounds that the pain was part of God's punishment of Eve for her act of disobedience in the Garden of Eden.

———— • ————

In King Canute's time, adulterous women had their ears and noses cut off.

Prostitutes in ancient Greece used to wear sandals with the words 'Follow Me' on the soles. Their potential customers read the footprints. The ancient Greeks believed there were two compartments in the womb: girls on the left, boys on the right.

———— • ————

Lord Byron had sex with his nanny at the age of nine – when *he* was nine, not the nanny.

———— • ————

A Chinese face-reader recently claimed that anyone with small ear-lobes was probably a bedroom bore with sexual hang-ups.

Dr Glen Wilson, a psychologist at the University of London, believes that men who leave their socks on during sex are showing signs of insecurity.

———— • ————

According to a recent survey only one per cent of the male population of France make love to their wives on a Monday.

———— • ————

Ancient Egyptian men rubbed crocodile dung into their phalluses to make them bigger.

I Don't Believe It!

Actress, Clara Bow, is alleged to have had sex with the entire football team of the University of California in Los Angeles.

———— • ————

A Roman doctor called Soranos concluded that the best method of contraception was for the woman to hold her breath at the crucial moment and afterwards sneeze violently.

———— • ————

Here are some good stories about queens –
the real ones of course!

Queen Elizabeth I lost all her teeth because of her passion for cakes. She spat a lot and loved swilling beer and was something of a flasher. The French Ambassador reported that, during a private audience, she insisted on pulling open the front of her white damask dress so that he could see her belly button.

———— • ————

Mary Queen of Scots brought her dog with her to her execution.

Anne Boleyn (who was thought by some to be a witch because she had six fingers on one hand), annoyed King Henry VIII by not producing sons. She also had a bad habit of throwing up the food she had eaten to make room for another binge. Her one concession to table manners was to hold a sheet in front of her face as she relieved her bulging stomach.

———— • ————

Queen Anne grew so fat she had to be raised and lowered through trap doors by means of ropes and pulleys. (By the way, all her 17 children pre-deceased her.)

———— • ————

Queen Christina of Sweden had a pathological fear of fleas. She had a four-inch cannon built to shoot them with.

The Queen of Bohemia introduced the custom of wearing shoes with toes so long that the ends had to be tied to her knees to prevent her tripping over them.

———— • ————

St Uncumber *almost* became a queen. She was the daughter of the King of Portugal – one of septuplets. Her father decided to marry her off to the King of Sicily but she would have none of it. In order to make herself repellent to her would-be husband, she grew a beard. Her father, not taking kindly to her disobedience, cut off her head. And if you don't believe me, there's a statue of her, complete with beard in King Henry VII's chapel in Westminster Abbey!

Catherine the Great of Russia prescribed sex six times a day as a cure for insomnia.

———— • ————

Cleopatra, the offspring of a brother and sister, married two of her brothers.

———— • ————

And finally . . . Queen Victoria kept a daily diary for 68 years. She had nine children and they gave her 64 grandchildren.

"You can't be tired. We've only had sex five times today."

I'm a bit like Groucho Marx, who famously wired this message: 'Please accept my resignation. I don't want to belong to any club which will accept me as a member.' But in America there's a society for everything.

You can become a card-carrying member of The National Prune Juice Packers Association. Or would you prefer to be a member of The Society for the Prevention of Calling Sleeping-Car Porters 'George'? (I couldn't have invented that!) Or there's The Society for the Prevention of the Practice of

Referring to a Bathroom as a John. Or one called The National Indignation Society. (If there was one in England, Victor Meldrew would be its president!)

———— • ————

There's The International Footprint Association, The Dairy Goat Council of America, The Oyster Shell Institute and – this is on the level – God's Garden Club.

———— • ————

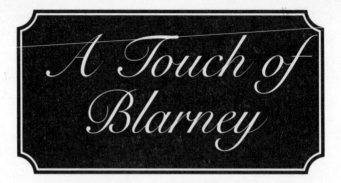

A Touch of Blarney

Scottish humour is pawky, dry and caustic.
Irish humour is warm and lovable. Here
are some of my favourite examples – true
stories all, I give you my word!

———— • ————

In a Galway court, the prosecuting counsel was
pressing a witness for the defence who was claim-
ing he had no evil motive in acquiring a gun.
'Come now,' said the prosecutor. 'On your solemn
oath, what did you get the weapon for?'

'On my solemn oath,' said the witness, 'I got it
for three shillings in Richardson's pawn-office.'

Irish country justice can be a little eccentric and is summed up by a Limerick judge who dismissed the accused with the words: 'You go from this court with no stain on your character other than that you have been acquitted by an Irish jury.'

———— • ————

At the end of the last century, a Kerry magistrate asked a farmer, who had chosen to conduct his own defence, if he was guilty or not guilty.

'Indeed, I'm innocent, your honour,' said the farmer. 'Sure, if I was guilty I'd have found me a lawyer.'

———— • ————

In a similar situation where the accused chose to defend himself, the judge warned him it would be wise to have a lawyer to represent him.

'I am not worried, your honour. I may have no counsel but I have several friends on the jury.'

Mr Justice Fitzgibbon used to take his dog into court with him. On one occasion, John Curran, a celebrated barrister, seeing that Fitzgibbon was stroking his dog, stopped in mid-sentence.

'Why have you stopped, Mr Curran?' said the judge.

'I thought your lordships were in consultation!' retorted Curran.

On another occasion, the judge dismissed Curran's argument with the words: 'If that be the law, Mr Curran, I will burn my law books.'

Curran answered: 'But read them first, my lord.'

———— • ————

On another occasion, a judge asked a jury how they could possibly have found a man guilty of theft when he had proved he was somewhere quite different. 'Ah!' said the foreman knowingly, 'but he would have done it if he had been there!'

*"It doesn't look very promising. The judge is always
influenced by his dog's opinion."*

Though Ireland was neutral in the Second World War, there were many Irish volunteers in the British army. In 1942, when an Irish soldier asked his platoon commander for compassionate leave to visit his wife, who was about to give birth, the officer said he could not as he had had a letter from the soldier's wife particularly asking him not to do so.

'By God sir,' said the soldier, 'I respect that entirely. You're as good a liar as I am any day. Sure, I was never married!'

———— • ————

A Wexford doctor was summoned to the house of a farmer whom he found to be suffering from pneumonia. The farmer was unable to explain it. 'I went to the fair at Enniscorthy yesterday,' he said. 'I walked home and when I got home I took off my hat and trousers and hung them on the back of the door and went to bed. When I woke up, I was lying in a ditch full of water and my hat and trousers were hanging in a tree.'

The poet Yeats was manager of the Abbey Theatre. One day, after many frustrating attempts to get the lighting right for a sunset scene, a deep red glow appeared along the back of the stage.

'That's it! That's exactly what I want,' said Yeats excitedly.

'Well, you can't have it,' said the electrician scrambling through a trap door onto the stage. 'The bloody theatre's on fire!'

———— • ————

You'd Better Believe It Because It's True

Did you know that Pontius Pilate was a Scot? I didn't but it's true. His father was governor of that part of the Roman Empire. Pilate was born at Fortingall near Dunkeld. As a Scot myself, I don't know whether to be proud or aghast!

I can feel a list of useless information coming on!

Only human beings sleep on their backs.

YOU'D BETTER BELIEVE IT
BECAUSE IT'S TRUE

The average person spends almost 12 years of his or her life watching television. (I suppose I ought to be grateful!)

———— • ————

In a year, a person's heart beats 40 million times.

———— • ————

70 per cent of living organisms in the world are bacteria.

———— • ————

The Sahara Desert is as large as America and getting bigger.

There's cyanide in apple pips.

———— • ————

Over three quarters of a potato is water.

———— • ————

Ice is lighter than water.

———— • ————

Much of Beethoven's best music was composed after he had gone deaf.

YOU'D BETTER BELIEVE IT
BECAUSE IT'S TRUE

Half of the world's area of land water is in Canada.

———— • ————

The bat is the only mammal that flies.

———— • ————

Karl Marx gave up working as a columnist on the *New York Tribune* in the mid-1800s when his salary was cut from $10 to $5.

———— • ————

There's a New Zealand reptile that can hold its breath for an hour.

Oysters change their sex according to the temperature of the water around them.

———— • ————

When the Washington Monument was opened to the public in 1888 the men took the lift but the women were made to climb the 897 steps. It was thought improper for men and women to share a lift and nobody seems to have thought of allowing the ladies some 'women only' rides in the lift.

———— • ————

President John F. Kennedy was the first president of the United States born in the twentieth century.

On 7 December, 1978 Diane Tuminaro gave birth to her second son exactly one year to the minute after the birth of her first.

———— • ————

Diamonds, contrary to the cliché, don't necessarily 'last forever'. When a diamond has just been mined it sometimes explodes.

———— • ————

Nightmare
Notices

On a building site:
**Night-watchman patrols this area
24-hours-a-day.**

———— • ————

In a factory:
Closing down, thanks to all our customers.

———— • ————

In a shop:
**Ears pierced while you wait. Pay for two and
get another one pierced free.**

NIGHTMARE NOTICES

In a garage:
Free estimates at almost no cost.

———— • ————

In a chemist:
We dispense with accuracy.

———— • ————

In a funeral parlour car park:
No exit.

———— • ————

In a laundrette:
Leave your clothes and go and enjoy yourself.

I Don't Believe It!

In a Travel Agent:
Why don't you go away?

———— • ————

In a restaurant:
Lunch served from 12.30 to mid-October.

———— • ————

In a foreign hotel:
**If you have any desires in the night, ring for
the chambermaid...**

———— • ————

In a newspaper small ads column:
**Happy home wanted for lovely dog. Will eat
anything – loves children.**

*"Excuse me, do you have any
children-flavoured dog food?"*

Newspaper Misprince
(oops!)

Victor Meldrew is often thoroughly disgusted by what he reads in the newspaper. He is particularly annoyed by misprints. Personally, I really enjoy the odd misprint. Here are a few of my favourites:

———— • ————

In an unfortunate error last week we said that Mr South was a member of the defective branch of the local police force. This should, of course, read 'detective' branch of the local police farce.

Apart from some scattered showers, there were only eight days in February without sin.

———— • ————

The annual Christmas party at Ashley Street School was hell yesterday afternoon.

———— • ————

Two Fast Germans escaped to West Berlin during Easter.

———— • ————

The bride wore a long white dress which fell to the floor.

I DON'T BELIEVE IT!

Decorator specializes in inferior work. Estimates free.

———— • ————

One of the newer MPs rushed across the floor to shake a clenched fish in the Prime Minister's face.

———— • ————

Repeat showing of *The Mayor of Casterbridge*: a threat in store for those who missed it last Sunday.

———— • ————

Firemen had a stiff bottle before the blaze was finally brought under control.

Last night, the home-coming World Cup squad waved goodbye to 35,000 hell-wishers.

———— • ————

And finally, from an Irish newspaper: 'In many parts of County Sligo hares are practically unknown because of the unreasonable laughter to which they had been subjected in recent years.' (You could say they died laughing.)

Even Nuttier Notices

I can't resist giving you a few more – all
genuine – 'Nutty Notices'.

———— • ————

On a luggage trolley at Singapore airport:
Not to be removed from Crewe station.

———— • ————

In a dress shop:
Wedding gear for all occasions.

In a hospital:
Dangerous drugs must be locked up with the Matron.

——— • ———

Outside a social club:
Closed tonight for special opening.

——— • ———

On a lane:
When you can't see this sign the river is under water.

——— • ———

On an optician's door:
If you can't read this come in.

I Don't Believe It!

In an employment agency:
Wanted: Ejection-seat tester.
Involves small amount of travelling.

———— • ————

In a hairdresser:
Haircuts half price today.
One only per customer.

———— • ————

On a lift:
Please do not use this lift when it is not working.

———— • ————

In a jeweller's shop:
Our gifts will not last long at these prices.

*"I do wish you wouldn't
bring your work home with you."*

I Don't Believe It!

In a dry cleaners in St Albans:
If you feel we have failed you in any way we shall be only too pleased to do it again at no extra charge.

———— • ————

In a hotel:
Ladies are requested not to have children in the Cocktail Room.

———— • ————

In another hotel:
Spend your honeymoon with us and we will guarantee it is the best you ever had.

———— • ————

Even Nuttier Notices

In a restaurant:
Steaks and chops are grilled
before our customers.

———— • ————

And one last one from a brochure
for a seaside hotel:
Unlike some resorts, the sea
comes right up to the shore.

Here are some things that aren't what they pretend to be:

The prairie dog is a rodent and so is the guinea pig which, apart from not being a pig, is not from Guinea. Fireflies aren't flies but beetles – as are glow worms.

———— • ————

Zebras have white stripes – not black ones.

———— • ————

Buffalo Bill didn't hunt buffalo but bison.

*"I used to be called 'Bison Bill' but my agent
thought 'Buffalo Bill' sounded better."*

I Don't Believe It!

Great Danes come from Germany.

———— • ————

The Hundred Years War lasted for a 114 years.

———— • ————

The Great Wall of China – contrary to legend – cannot be seen from the moon.

———— • ————

The American nickel is made not of nickel but copper.

The primrose has nothing to do with roses.

———— • ————

An ostrich puts its head in the sand not to hide but to cover its eggs or look for food.

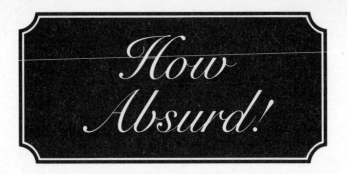

Here is a gathering of absurd – but true –
stories except that they make me shake my
head at the strangeness of the world!

———— • ————

A Parisian couple committed joint suicide in their
wedding gear. They left this note: 'We are killing
ourselves because we are too happy. We do not
need more money. We have good health. We
adore each other but would rather descend into the
grave together while we are still so happy.'

And there is the case of the flat-chested bank clerk who stuffed her brassiere with money to impress her boyfriend with her vital statistics – at least, that was her story!

———— • ————

The Bible doesn't mention Eve eating an apple – nor Jonah being swallowed by a whale.

———— • ————

Lord Charles Beresford – this was over a century ago – newly married, burst into what he thought was his bride's room stark naked and calling cock-a-doodle-do. Unfortunately, it turned out to be the room of the Bishop of Chester and his wife.

The eccentric and reclusive millionaire, Howard Hughes, used to store his urine indefinitely in large metal containers.

——— • ———

There have been more than 9000 books written about Abraham Lincoln.

——— • ———

In Buenos Aires, a cat ran up a tree and stayed there for six years having three lots of kittens while she was up there.

——— • ———

In 1979, a woman from Northamptonshire went to her doctor to have her ears syringed . . . and the doctor was startled when a baby tooth fell out. It had been there for 30 years. The woman had, as a child, put the tooth under her pillow but the tooth fairy had never come.

"I'm the tooth fairy, sorry I'm late."

Here are eight sentences that, backwards or forwards, mean the same (though that's not much!)

Dogs a devil deified, deified lived as God.

——— • ———

I roamed under it as a tired nude Maori.

——— • ———

A man, a plan, a canal, – Panama.

Trap part if I trap part.

———— • ————

Won't lovers revolt now.

———— • ————

Live not on evil.

———— • ————

Was it a car or a cat I saw.

More Unbelievable Stories

From the *East Africa Standard*, 1975: Nanyuki farmer seeks lady owning tractor with view to companionship and possible tractor. Send picture of tractor to Box 132, Nanyuki.

———— • ————

In 1910, a man was arrested for speeding in Cardiff. He was doing ten miles an hour.

Surgeons in Durham operated on a psychiatric patient and found in his stomach 336 halfpennies, 25 sixpences, 17 threepenny bits, 11 pennies and four shillings. (Now try and convert that to present day coinage!)

———— • ————

When Jimmy Simmond escaped from prison in 1985, he hitched a lift into the nearest town. Unfortunately for him . . . it was a police car. However, talking of bad luck – what about the two burglars in the north of England? They found a camera and took pictures of each other but . . . left it behind when they left with the booty.

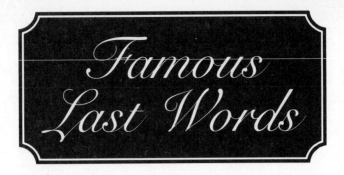

Famous Last Words

I don't believe it – I mean that famous people on their respective death beds say wise and witty things but here are some I would like to believe were really said.

———— • ————

Kings live and die in public so it is hardly surprising their last words are written down. King Charles II is supposed to have apologized: 'I have been a most unconscionable time a-dying, but I beg you to excuse it.'

I don't think any dying man could say 'unconscionable'. I prefer to think he said, remembering his favourite mistress: 'Let not poor Nelly starve.'

George V may have said: 'How is the empire?' but surely such a pointless question must have been put into his mouth by some pompous court official. I prefer to think he said: 'Bugger Bognor.' This was in response to a fatuous doctor telling him he would soon be convalescing at the seaside.

———— • ————

Benjamin Disraeli refused Queen Victoria's kind offer to visit him on his deathbed saying: 'No it is better not. She will only ask me to take a message to Albert.'

———— • ————

Oscar Wilde dying in a Paris hotel is said to have asked for champagne and remarked: 'I am dying, as I have lived, beyond my means.' Or did he say, as some claim, 'Either that wallpaper goes or I do.'

Voltaire, another great wit, was visited by a priest on his deathbed:

'Who sent you, Monsieur l'Abbe?' asked the old atheist.

'God himself, Monsieur Voltaire,' the priest answered.

'Ah, my dear sir,' replied the dying man, 'and where are your credentials?'

———— • ————

(Voltaire had said at the funeral of a certain noble-man: 'He was a great patriot, a humanitarian, a loyal friend – provided, of course, that he really is dead!')

———— • ————

It was Mark Twain who cabled a New York news-paper that had reported he was dead: REPORT OF MY DEATH GREATLY EXAGGERATED.

The poet, Walter de la Mare, lay very ill. His daughter asked if she could get him anything – fruit perhaps, or flowers?

'No,' he muttered, 'too late for fruit, too soon for flowers.'

———— • ————

And finally, Dorothy Parker – when the doctor said she must give up drinking or she would be dead within three months, whispered: 'Promises, promises . . .'

(She had once told a friend who could not bring herself to put down her ailing cat: 'Try curiosity.')

As a Scot, I have always found the English bewildering, particularly in politics, but the English 'stiff upper lip' in times of danger is always to be admired. It's summed up for me in this story of the Battle of Waterloo. Lord Paget, Wellington's second in command, was hit by a cannon-ball as the two men watched the battle.

Paget turned to Wellington and exclaimed: 'Good God, my leg's been struck off.' Wellington calmly rode his horse round in front of Paget and said: 'Good God, man, so it has.'

There's only one response to such sangfroid: **'I don't believe it!'**.